LIGHTS! CAMERA! ACTION!

HOW A MOVIE IS MADE

BY GAIL GIBBONS

THOMAS Y. CROWELL   NEW YORK

For Bonnie Ancliffe

Lights! Camera! Action!
How a Movie Is Made
Copyright © 1985 by Gail Gibbons
Printed in the U.S.A. All rights reserved.
10 9 8 7 6 5 4 3 2 1

Library of Congress Cataloging in Publication Data
Gibbons, Gail.
   Lights! Camera! Action!

   Summary: A step-by-step description of how a movie is
made, including writing the script, casting, rehearsing,
creating the scenery and costumes, editing the film,
and attending the premier.
   1. Moving pictures—Production and direction—
Juvenile literature. [1. Motion pictures—Production
and direction] I. Title.
PN1995.9.P7G44 1985   791.43'023   85-47536
ISBN 0-690-04476-3
ISBN 0-690-04477-1 (lib. bdg.)

Special thanks to Robert Glass of Todd-AO Corp., Los Angeles, California; Victor Pisano of NightOwl
Productions, Salem, Massachusetts.
Also thanks to DeForest Research of MGM/UA Entertainment Co., Culver City, California; Harold Rand and
Amy Waterman of Astoria Studios, Astoria, New York; Michael Gerin of Cine 60, Inc., New York, New York;
Luis Zapata of The Editing Machine, New York, New York; George Darrell of BHP Inc., Chicago, Illinois; Ron
Little of CFI, Hollywood, California; Michael John Peters of Quad Eight/Westrex, San Fernando, California; and
Robert Eberenz of Magna-Tech Electronic Co., Inc., New York, New York.

The story is perfect! It is exactly what the movie producers have been looking for. They want to take the story and make it into a movie.

The producers hire the people they will need to get started.

It could take millions of dollars to make the movie. The producers describe their project to people who might lend them money. That's how they get their "financial backing."

A major movie studio also likes the project. They will back the movie, too. And when the movie is finished, they will rent out copies to movie theaters.

Step 1: Pre-production…

Now the work begins. The producers hire a scriptwriter. It takes a long time to turn a story into a script, or screenplay. All the dialogue for the actresses and actors is written in the script along with technical directions for lighting, camera angles, and scene changes.

Next, the casting director is hired. She finds actors and actresses to play the leading parts. Sometimes the people chosen are very famous...stars!

There are tryouts for the smaller parts.

The producers need to find just the right locations for the different scenes. Then the production manager makes a schedule for filming them.

Sketches are made.

The pre-production crew is bigger now.
The different departments work to get everything ready.
The costume designers, the lighting technicians,

the property department, the set designers,

the sound technicians, and the special effects department
rush to meet the production deadline.

The actresses and actors rehearse...

and rehearse their lines.

Finally, after months of work, everyone and everything is ready. It is time for the different scenes to be filmed.

They will not be shot in the order of the script. All the scenes in the same location, or on the same set, will be shot together. It is easier and costs less that way. When the filming is over, the scenes will be put together in order again.

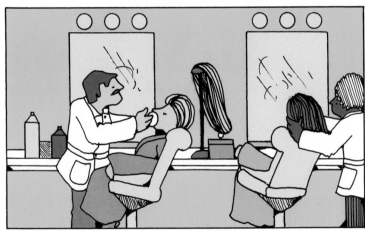

The actresses and actors arrive early each morning.
In the dressing rooms, makeup artists and hair stylists
get them ready for the day's shooting. Wardrobe assistants
help them into their costumes.

Meanwhile, over on the set, the camera operators are in position. The sound technicians are adjusting their equipment. The lighting technicians, called gaffers, have set up the lights.

The actors and actresses come in.

The scene is rehearsed one last time.

Step 2: Production…

Everything looks right.
The director gives a signal. The assistant director yells,
"Quiet on the set!"

Production begins.
Lights! Camera! Action!

The director yells, "Cut!" Somebody missed a line.

They reshoot the scene until it is perfect.
"Print it!" the director yells. He likes the take.

Film processor

At the end of the day, all the takes are rushed to the film processing lab to be printed.

Each day's film is called a daily. Every morning the producers and director view the dailies from the day before.

Step 3: Post-production...

Once all the scenes have been shot, the film editors take over. They go through the reels and reels of film and select what they need. If it isn't just right, it is out.

The edited film is spliced together in the order of the scenes in the script.

The producers and director view the film. They all agree—it's just what they want. It works!

Dubbing console

Next, music must be added to the sound track.
A composer is hired. The music he creates will set the
mood for the film.

Any mistakes in the dialogue can be corrected now.
Mixers put the music, dialogue, and sound effects together.
Then the complete sound track will be added to the film.

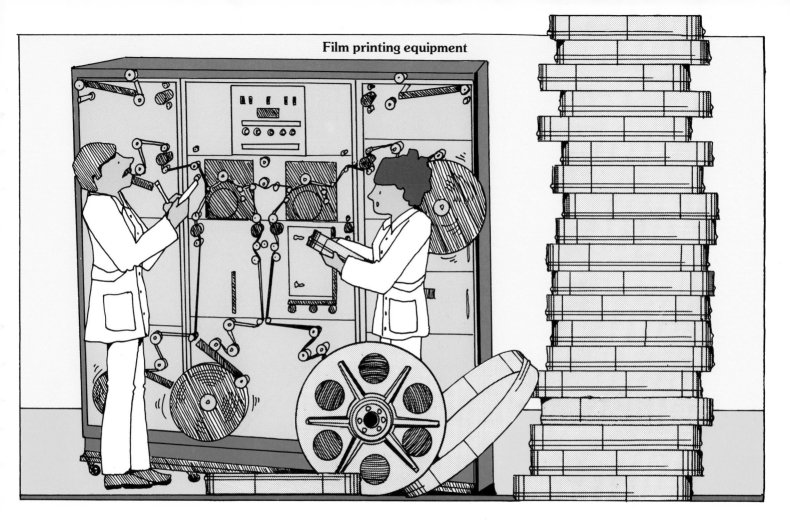

Film printing equipment

The movie is completed.

The first print, called an answer print, is made and given one final check. Then thousands of copies, called release prints, are made.

The movie studio will rent out these copies to the movie theaters. For months, the studio has been advertising the movie and stirring up interest with a big publicity campaign.

The premier showing is held at a big city theater. The stars are there. All the people who made the movie are there, too.

Fans and movie critics come to the glamorous event.

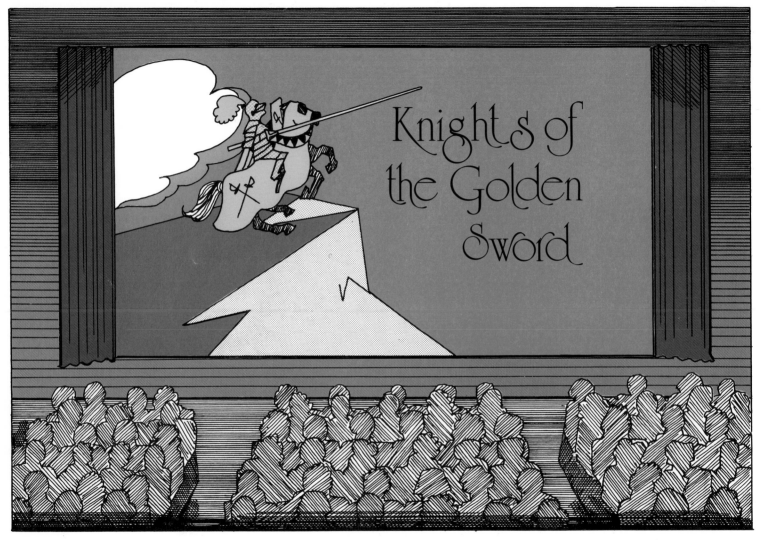

The audience waits.
The lights go out and the movie begins.